ICEBREAKERS

How to Empower, Inspire and Motivate Your Team, Through Step-by-Step Activities That Boost Confidence, Resilience and Create Happier Individuals

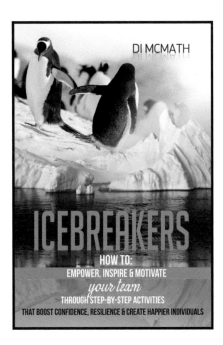

Di McMath

Dreamstone Publishing 2015

www.dreamstonepublishing.com

Copyright © 2015 Di McMath and Platinum Potential

ISBN: 1925165388

ISBN-13: 978-1-925165-38-8

www.platinumpotential.com.au

DISCLAIMER

This representation of ICEBREAKERS: How to Empower, Inspire and Motivate Your Team, Through Step-by-Step Activities That Boost Confidence, Resilience and Create Happier Individuals is the intellectual property of the Author Di McMath founder of Platinum Potential. It is sold with the understanding that it is not a resource to provide any substitute for psychological, medical, legal or any other professional advice.

No warrantees or guarantees are implied, and the Author takes no responsibility or liability for any unforseen outcomes or results from any underlying psychological issues that the participants may have (physical, psychological, emotional, financial or commercial damages, including but not limited to, special, incidental, consequential or other damages). Our views and rights are the same: You are responsible for your own choices, actions, and results.

Activities may be modified for suitability at the discretion of the reader, however the author takes no responsibility for any adverse outcomes. This book is not meant to be used, nor should it be used, to diagnose or treat any medical condition. For diagnosis or treatment of any medical problem, consult your own physician. Readers should be aware that the websites listed in this book may change.

ACKNOWLEDGEMENTS

This collection of activities would not have come about if it wasn't for the wonderful inspiring advice, support and honesty of my dear friend Emma Walkinshaw. Thank you my friend – for encouraging me to believe in myself, for our numerous chats, and for teaching me that challenges can be overcome if you have a good 'chinwag' and a laugh!

To my beautiful daughter Ella - for continually inspiring me to be my *better self* every day, and for your kind, loving, sweet soul. I love you always, and grow prouder of you every day.

For Ric, my *rock*, my soulmate, and my best friend - thank you for being everything that you are. You warm my heart every day.

My wonderful personal mentor - 'Uncle Geoff', for your genuine support, humour and phenomenal guidance- you're a star!

For my loving sister Jacqui, thank you for your endless encouragement and belief.

For my amazing friends who've supported me throughout my journey. There are too many to mention, but you all know who you are, and I am so grateful to have you in my life.

For my neighbour and friend Carmel, thanks for being my *technical guru* and such a great support!

For my high school teacher, soccer coach, mentor and friend Brett Green - for teaching me that dedication, persistence and loving what you do — is totally worth it, and that fulfilment comes from helping others to shine.

A big thank you to Anthony Robbins — for *unknowingly* being my mentor and guide for almost two decades - your teachings constantly drive me to *'Live with Passion'*.

Last but not least, to my late mum 'Kay' - for being such a wonderful inspiration and role model, as well as for continuing to show your love and support in spiritual ways. I love you always, and will continue to endeavour to make you proud.

xox

What people are saying about 'ICEBREAKERS'

How to Empower, Inspire and Motivate Your Team, Through Step-by-Step Activities That Boost Confidence, Resilience and Create Happier Individuals

" I'm really blown away by your book, and I think any principal would be foolish not to implement this into their school, especially with the climate of bullying these days. This would really lift team morale amongst teachers and students and that would be something that would make my heart sing! "

Lauren Massey - Teacher –

★

" What a difference just doing <u>one</u> activity made with our family! We learnt so many wonderful things about each other, and in just three days – there has been less yelling, more laughing, and a lot more talking! Thank you for knowing how to open our eyes and hearts! "

Isla Chambers - Mother of three, aged 7, 5 & 3yrs-

★

"In my view THIS is the type of book that I had wished that I had when I was a trainer. To be honest, I'm happy that I have it now. It's like the **TRAINERS BIBLE** of activities for all types of groups! It's set out perfectly, and, more importantly, so simple to understand! Di provides a simple and extremely practical tool for initial bonding and - honesty works every time!"

Emma Walkinshaw

– Former National Training Manager for 'Brighter Futures'

★

TABLE of CONTENTS

INTRODUCTION

This book was something that was probably ridiculously obvious to my subconscious mind for a long time, but took a while to pop into my consciousness!

Yet once it did, it literally took about four weeks to write.

I had just finished developing a three day workshop for schools, when I began having an informal chat with my daughter's school principal about it.

Her response was honest and I have to say that it 'burst my bubble' at the time, but after thinking about it and *reframing* it – she burst it in a good way.

She said that teachers would *'freak out'* at the amount of **_time_** it was, and wonder how they could squeeze that around their curriculum.

After all, three *hours* was difficult to squeeze in let alone three days!

So that night, whilst chatting with a friend on the phone and talking about the principal's statement….the idea of this book arose.

Basically the workshop, that I had put together, was a collection of activities designed to help improve self-esteem, build confidence, team building, and self-*empower* individuals and their teams – so why not just provide them with the information and guidance in the form of a book, and let them implement it when they feel like they need to?

Then the ideas kept flowing.

These activities can be adapted to people of all ages and different situations, so I thought that I'd just add more and potentially help a whole range of people!

Teachers, Coaches, Trainers, Facilitators, Workplace Managers, Sporting teams, Parents, virtually *anybody!*

So, here it is.

A step by step guide to empowering your team as a whole *and* individually!

I've been inspired by so many of my mentors that I'm yet to meet, and this collection of activities is a testament to them that their teachings have not only been a huge influence on me, but will continue to have a positive *ripple effect* on the world.

Some activities are a direct reflection of what they teach, and some have been inspired as a *result* of their teachings.

Even my daughter Ella helped to create an activity in here, so I thank you all for helping to infuse such 'inspiration' into the lives of our world's future.

May you enjoy this collection of inspiring activities, implement them into your amazing team, and watch the results filter into every area of their lives *and* your organisation.

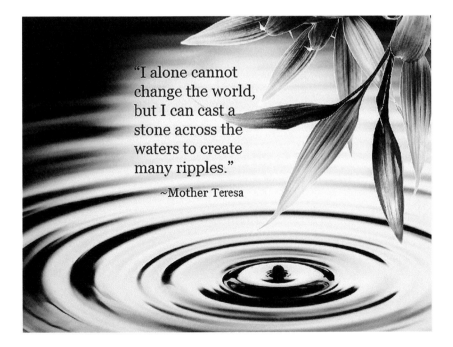

"I alone cannot change the world, but I can cast a stone across the waters to create many ripples."

~Mother Teresa

How to Use This Book

Each activity has a ***purpose*** based on what the author perceives that the intended outcome will be. Many activities cover a combination of purposes. ***Ultimately, all activities are intended to give a positive outcome.***

An Explanation of the 'Purpose' – Codes / Abbreviations

SE: SELF ESTEEM.
This activity can help to build participants self-esteem.

C: CONFIDENCE.
This activity can help to build participants confidence.

SA: SELF AWARENESS.
This activity can give the participants self-awareness.

R: RESILIENCE.
This activity can help to build participants resilience.

H: HAPPINESS.
This activity can help to increase participants overall happiness.

TB: TEAM BUILDING.
This activity assists in positive team building.

LB: LEADERSHIP BUILDING.
This activity helps participants in leadership building.

GS: GOAL SETTING.
This activity assists in positive goal setting.

Each activity also gives an indication of the approximate duration.

Eg: If you only have 5mins to spare and feel like your group may need an activity that will help to assist in positive team building…

- Look at the activities 'purpose' section on the next page and search for **'TB'**.
- Go to the column with the heading **'Approx. Duration'**
- Find the corresponding activity that takes approximately 5mins.
- Turn to that page number.

Bonus Content

Some activities have '**(*see appendix for Bonus Downloadable Sheets)**' for additional resources with the activity. These resources are available to be ***downloaded*** in PDF format from the **'Bonus Content'** links provided in the appendix.

Note:

References and Bibliography for the activities can be found at the back of the book.

Table of Activities, Purpose and Duration

Activities Grouped by Purpose.

Although you would have noticed, in the table on the preceding pages, that the majority of activities have a *combined purpose,* I have summarised them into categories based on the **main purpose** for which you may wish to do each activity.

The headings are based upon each *purpose* that the activities in the book cover.

SE: SELF ESTEEM.

I Am

Affirmation Exercise

Letter to Yourself

The Compliment Chair

C: CONFIDENCE.

Creating Empowering Beliefs

Achieving Success

SA: SELF AWARENESS.

The Power of Our Language

Negative Rubbish Dump

The Power of Tone and Expression

Creative Questioning

Emotional Reactions

R: RESILIENCE.

The Power of 'Telling Your Truth'

Keeping Dreams Alive

Burst your OWN Bubbles

Achievement Board

H: HAPPINESS.

Balance Sheet of Life

Breathing Positivity

The Power of Journals

Little Jar of Fulfilment

TB: TEAM BUILDING.

Guess Who

Interesting Commonalities

LB: LEADERSHIP BUILDING.

Lead with Dancing

Which Hat will you Wear?

GS: GOAL SETTING.

Pin the Star on the Target

Vision Boards

The Activities

Have you ever had to facilitate a group/team where you wished you could just click your fingers and there was an instant lift of energy in the room?

Or have you ever wished that you could allow your group/team to discover their own potential and see how amazing they really are – and *can* be?

The activities in this book are a wonderful collection of *'ICEBREAKERS'* that are aimed at giving individuals and groups/teams a variety of uplifting life skills, which – when used on a regular basis, can provide a solid foundation for positive growth.

Every group/team needs to set goals to know what it is that they want to achieve.

Every group/team needs to be aware of their strengths and weaknesses.

Every group/team needs to have confidence in order to grow.

Every group/team needs to learn resilience for when they encounter setbacks.

Every group/team needs to build a healthy relationship with the members of their group/team.

Every group/team needs leaders that can empower and inspire others to be the best that they can be.

As we are all aware, all groups and teams are made up of individuals. So the activities in this book also have a strong focus on individual growth.

When a person feels like they are 'growing' they are fulfilling a basic human need, and *that* contributes to their level of life fulfilment, and ultimately their happiness. When an individual is happy, then that can *infuse* into those around them.

I encourage you to use these activities and to be creative with them. Nothing is *set in concrete* – so there are no *hard and fast* rules. Use them as a guide, and as a tool to open your *own* mind to creating ways to *'Empower'* your team.

Enjoy!

1.

The 'I AM' Exercise

Approx. Duration

- 10-20 minutes

Resources Required

- A4 pieces of paper with thick plain borders printed on them (approx. 3cm in width) **(*see appendix for Bonus Downloadable sheets)**
- A photo of each participant (preferably torso – up)(Can be done *post* activity)
- Glue
- Pens (colourful = optional)

> **Preparation**

Each participant glues their own photo into the middle of the piece of paper, and writes the words 'I AM…' on the top of the page.

This is what the paper should look like.

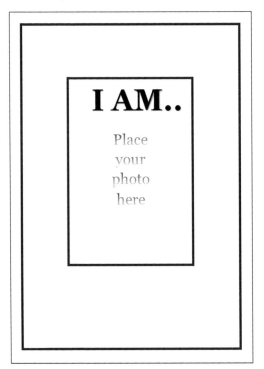

Activity

Beginning with the words 'I am', participants are to write down words within the border of the A4 piece of paper, that complete the sentence – **in a positive sense**. (Eg: I am – *kind, thoughtful, considerate* etc).

The finished piece can be displayed somewhere when the participant will see it every day, and get used to reading it.

Purpose

Self Esteem / Confidence / Self Awareness / Resilience / Happiness

The more positive things we search for, the more we will find.

If we have a reference to remind us on a daily basis, it may not only provide increased confidence and self -esteem, but it trains the mind to search for the positive things in our life.

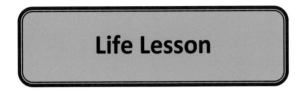

'I am in charge of how I feel, and today I'm choosing happiness'

-Shawny-

Affirmation Exercise

Approx. Duration

- 5 minutes

Resources Required

- Completed 'I am' list from previous exercise

Preparation

Participants are to stand in front of a mirror with their 'I am' list.

Activity

- Participants are to stand in front of a mirror (or have a mirror held in front of them), and one by one, whilst looking at themselves in the mirror, read out loud the list that they made.

- Participants are encouraged to be aware of their physiology whilst they are standing in front of the mirror and doing their affirmations. Using encouraging gestures (eg: smiling, tone of voice, pointing at themselves in the mirror, hand on their heart etc) when they say the statements.

- At first, it may seem 'fake' or 'awkward' for participants to say these to themselves, but by doing this on a daily basis it will become easier and more comfortable to do.

- Participants may find it helpful to think of a time that relates to the statement that they are saying (eg: "I am kind"….and they think of when they did something nice for someone).

- It is recommended that they do this activity on a daily basis for at least 21days.

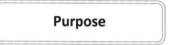

Purpose

Self Esteem / Confidence / Self Awareness / Resilience / Happiness

Affirmations on a consistent basis, are like implanting a belief. Participants have come up with their own 'I am' statements, and this is a way of imprinting more positive statements and in turn –they begin to believe what they are saying. By using their senses of sight, hearing and touch, and recalling a reference to each statement, it allows individuals to become more associated with what they are saying.

Life Lesson

'Repetition is the mother of skill'

- Anthony Robbins-

Creating Empowering Beliefs

Approx. Duration

- 10-15 minutes

Resources Required

- Pen
- Paper
- Ruler
- Whiteboard and Whiteboard marker

Preparation

Print copies of the Disempowering to Empowering sheet **(*see appendix for Bonus Downloadable sheets).** Below is an example of the sheet.

Disempowering Statement	Empowering Statement
Change to:	
1.	
2.	
3.	
4.	
5.	
6.	
7.	
8.	
9.	
10.	

Activity

- Each participant is to write down, in the columns provided, the disempowering statements they currently believe about themselves (eg: I am fat, I am ugly etc).

- In the 'Empowering Belief' column, they are to write down the opposite to their 'disempowering belief' statement (Eg: If disempowering belief is 'I am fat', they could change it to an empowering belief like: 'I am on my road to a healthy body, I am beautiful in my own skin' etc).

- Then each participant is to find a partner to do the activity with.

- Instruct the participants to turn to their partner, stick one finger in one nostril and repeat the following 5 x :

(The Facilitator is to write this statement on the whiteboard for the participants to repeat).....

"I used to believe that____ (state the limiting belief) __and I now <u>know</u> that that is <u>untrue!!!</u>

I now believe that <u>(state the positive version to the limiting belief)</u>."

(expletives such as 'Bull#!*#' may be used for appropriate audience – eg: adults)

- Now participants are to say it again 5x each, but this time in a 'Chipmunk' voice, and with both fingers in their nose.

  Actions such as dancing on the spot can be added.

Purpose

Self Esteem / Resilience / Self Awareness

The aim is for participants to realise that their 'limiting belief' sounds ridiculous, and it 'confuses' their mind.

It's like scratching an old CD and replacing it with a new song.

Saying the new belief with real 'conviction' is **vital** to this exercise.

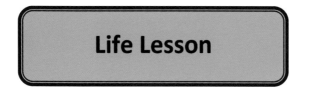

'Your <u>beliefs</u> become your <u>thoughts</u>,
Your thoughts become your <u>words</u>,
Your words become your <u>actions</u>,
Your actions become your <u>habits</u>,
Your habits become your <u>values</u>,
Your values become your <u>destiny</u>.'

-Mahatma Gandhi-

The Power of 'Telling Your Truth'

Approx. Duration

- 45-60 minutes

Resources Required

- Pen
- Notepads
- Backpack
- 1kg – 5kg Weights
- Matches OR a helium balloon and a normal balloon (number of balloons is determined by the number of participants. 2 of each may be needed for larger groups).

Preparation

This activity can be done two ways. If it is not safe for the group or it is not permitted to burn the paper, then the balloon technique can be used.

- Participants are to write down in depth, a secret or lie (theirs or others) that they have been keeping to themselves. They are to fold the piece of paper into a little piece and put it in their pocket for now.

- Using the backpack, the facilitator is to ask the participants one at a time – **"How heavy is this secret/lie that you are keeping?"** Using the weights, the participant is to put the amount of weights in the backpack that they feel is 'weighing them down'.

- The facilitator asks the person to put the backpack on, and try walking around with it.

- The facilitator asks questions like; "What would it feel like if you could lighten the load? What would be ways that you could do that?" Encourage a discussion.

- Then, after some participants have shared stories about the 'heaviness' of their loads (those that chose to), the facilitator encourages all of the participants to get the notes out of their pockets and stuff them into the balloons (yet to be blown up).

- Once all of the notes of the secrets / lies are in the balloon, the facilitator blows it up and ties it to the string of the helium balloon.

- Everyone is to then go outside into an open space, and the facilitator *discusses the power of telling your truth, and how freeing it can be when you do – then you won't have to carry around so much 'heavy weight upon your shoulders'.*

- The balloons are then let go.

  If notes are able to be burnt (instead of letting the balloons go), then that is another way of 'releasing' the heavy burden

- Discuss

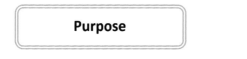

Purpose

Resilience / Self Awareness / Happiness

This activity can give participants the realisation that *holding onto* secrets and lies can be **emotionally heavy.**

The more truthful and authentic we are to ourselves and others, the more free we feel.

Be truthful to yourself, be truthful to others, and you will feel the *flow* of life.

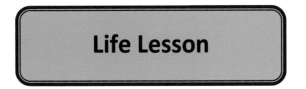

'If you tell the truth, you don't have to remember anything'

-Mark Twain-

Letter to Yourself

Approx. Duration

- 15-20 minutes

Resources Required

- Paper
- Pen
- Envelopes
- Stamps
- Softly playing inspirational music in the background (***see appendix for a suggested Play list**).

Preparation

Consider the timing carefully for this exercise - it is best done straight after an activity or discussion where participants have been discussing all of the *good / positive* things about themselves.

This activity has more effect when the letters are physically sent to the participants in the mail some time later.

Activity

Participants are initially guided through this imagery process by the facilitator:

*"Just for a moment, I'd like you to close your eyes and **imagine** that you are in this present moment, but you are able to 'rise' <u>way up</u> above yourself so that you are sitting on a soft, puffy peaceful little cloud and you are looking down upon yourself sitting here in this ***<u>classroom/room/building</u> (wherever your current location is).***

That's it....just rise away way up into the clouds so that you're sitting on your very own cloud, and seeing life as it currently is.

See what you're doing down here, from a different view – a 'special' view, a view that holds no judgement, no criticism, only love and kindness.

Now, looking at yourself from this position, you can also view your 'timeline' – the life that's already been, the life that you're currently in, and the life that is yet to come.

Just take a moment to be grateful for all of the moments and events that have led you to be in this place right now.

*What is it that you are grateful for, or **could** be grateful for about yourself? All the past achievements, accomplishments, decisions you've made that have led you to becoming the person that you are right now.*

The lessons you've learnt from events in your life – the good, and even the 'challenging' events...they've all got learnings that we can take from having them happen. Just take a moment to notice what you're grateful for.

*Take a big deep breath now....and just notice all of the things that you could be proud of yourself for. Or if you **wanted** to feel proud, what could you feel proud of?*

*As you're sitting up there on your little soft puffy cloud, just flood yourself with all the wonderful, kind, proud, happy, funny, loving thoughts about yourself that come into your mind and body. Just imagine, and let your mind run free - let them flow freely into your mind...even the thoughts that you would **like** to have about yourself.*

Just notice what those wonderful thoughts are. You may even like to forgive yourself for anything that you can see from up here – which you have now realised that you may have been a bit hard on yourself for. Whatever it is, make sure you stay in that non-judgemental, loving, kind, state.

Open your eyes.....”

Now, participants are asked to write down all of the wonderful thoughts that they've just experienced from being in that higher position, in the form of a letter to their current self. Still imagining that they are writing from their higher self, to their current self (3rd person – eg: Dear _____).

Once finished, they are to write their name and address on a stamped self-addressed envelope that is provided.

Now closing your eyes again...

*"Just imagine again, that you are still sitting on that soft, puffy cloud. Now, having noticed all of the wonderful things about yourself, I'd like you to just put your hand on your heart and just **know** that this kind and loving higher perspective of yourself is **always available**. It's there to serve you for your highest good.*

So as you slowly float down from the cloud, back into your current position – just feel how light you feel, and how warm and fulfilled after having now seen – a beautiful perspective of yourself."

Open your eyes.

The Facilitator is to take the letters, and post them at a random time in the future.

Purpose

Self Esteem / Resilience / Confidence / Self Awareness / Happiness

This is a wonderful exercise that allows participants to view their life or situation from a different perspective.

Capturing all of the kind and loving things that participants write to themselves in this moment, is a wonderful gift when they randomly receive it in the mail and a great reminder that they can easily see themselves or situations from a different view.

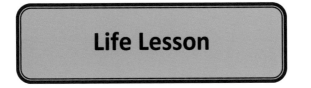

'*If you change the way you look at things, the things you look at change*'

-Wayne Dyer-

6.

The Power of Our Language

Approx. Duration

- 10-15 minutes

Resources Required

- Internet connection – 'YouTube'

  https://www.youtube.com/watch?v=iu9P167HLsw

  'How frequency (your words) can change water or human behaviour – Dr Masaru Emoto'

- Or: print out the water crystal pictures from http://www.masaru-emoto.net/english/water-crystal.html

Preparation

Participants are to be able to visualise the YouTube video clip from where they are seated.

Activity

Show the YouTube video clip (listed in the Resources for this exercise), or Google the pictures to show the class whilst you give an explanation of what the experiments were.

> ## Purpose

Self Awareness

Dr Masaru Emoto (a Japanese Doctor of Alternative Medicine) carried out a series of experiments where he realised that it was in the frozen crystal form, that water showed us its true nature.

He has gained worldwide acclaim through his ground breaking research and discovery, that water is deeply connected to our individual and collective consciousness. Positive, compassionate words comfort and heal; negative words and insults hurt.

Until recently, we knew this only because we could feel it, now we can actually see it. The experimental work of Dr. Emoto found that when we look at water in its frozen crystalized form, we can confirm the healing power of beautiful music, positive thinking, uplifting speech, and prayer.

With the human body made up of approximately 50-60% of water (with an infant even being approx. 73%), it is thought that uplifting words (both verbal and non-verbal) would have positive benefits at a cellular level.

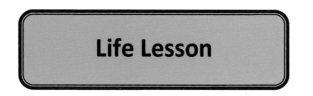

'Kind words can be short and easy to speak, but the echoes can be endless'

-Mother Teresa-

Negative Rubbish 'Dump'

Approx. Duration

- 5 minutes to prepare the rubbish bin
- < 5 minutes to explain the activity

Resources Required

- Rubbish bin
- Paper
- Marker Pen (Or print out the words from computer and laminate the sign)
- Sticky tape

Preparation

Using a computer to type it or marker pen to write it, print out the words **'Negative Rubbish'** and stick it on the side of a plastic rubbish bin. You can laminate it if you would like to make it neater, and reuse it.

Activity

At the start of a lesson (and anytime during the lesson if required), explain to participants that all of their negative thoughts, frustrations, anger and built up 'unwanted feelings' can simply be thrown into the rubbish bin provided.

Ask participants to take a moment to **be aware** of their current *negative rubbish* that they may be carrying, take a deep breath as they close their eyes – then as they exhale, imagine those negative thoughts and feelings coming out of them and they are screwing them up in a ball like a scrap bit of paper. Then **throw it / slam dunk it** into the bin provided.

Purpose

Self Awareness

A lot of the time, we aren't consciously aware of the negative thoughts / feelings that we are carrying around and are really *weighing us down* or giving off *bad energy* to those around us.

This activity helps participants to be consciously aware of their thoughts, and allows them to make a choice to get rid of them.

Participants are encouraged to also do this when they leave their workplace at the end of the day, and especially before they enter their home at night so that any 'negative rubbish' that they have picked up during the day – is not carried into other areas of their life.

Life Lesson

'You can't live a positive life with a negative mind'

-Unknown-

Balance Sheet of Life

Approx. Duration

- 20-30 minutes

Resources Required

- Piece of paper
- Pen
- Ruler

Preparation

All participants are to receive an *'Assets & Liabilities' sheet'* (*see appendix for Bonus Downloadable sheets)

The Sheets will look like this:

Balance Sheet Of Life	
ASSETS	**LIABILITIES**
Your world becomes brighter when you focus on your 'Assets', and be thankful for them ☺	

Activity

Participants are asked to write down all of their 'assets' in life. Not necessarily 'monetary assets', but more so 'things that they could be grateful for'. Eg: "I am loved, I am healthy, I have a wonderful family, I have food in the fridge," etc. ***The aim is to place real emphasis on the 'asset' column.***

In the 'liabilities' column, participants write down what they would consider to be 'liabilities' in their life.

Then, there is a discussion about what was learnt by doing that activity.

The facilitator is then to ***challenge a few of the 'liabilities'*** and show them how things can be turned into an *asset* instead of a liability. Eg: Liability = "I still haven't finished my house renovations" – could be turned into an asset such as: "I have enough money for renovating my house! Or I <u>have</u> a house to live in! Some people don't!"

Purpose

Resilience / Self Awareness / Happiness

When we look at our lives and immediately focus on what we *don't* have / don't want, we tend to *snowball* the thought and keep focusing on those negative things. Yet when you **start with the positives (*the assets*)** you tend to **look** and find more, with ease! With good guidance from the facilitator, this activity forces us to *change our perspective* when we think about our 'liabilities'.

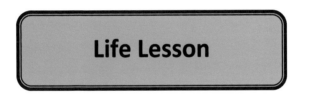

Life Lesson

'A negative thinker sees a difficulty in every opportunity.
A positive thinker sees an opportunity in every difficulty'

-Unknown-

Breathing Positivity

Approx. Duration

- 5-10 minutes

Resources Required

- A balloon for each participant

Preparation

Participants are to find a space standing up, where they are not crowding each other

---

Activity

Each participant is given a balloon.

The participants are to stand in a line all facing the same way.

The Facilitator guides the participants through this imagery process:

"I'd like you to imagine that all of your negative thoughts that are in your life right now…..are sitting at the bottom of your lungs.

Close your eyes if you need to, and just breathe in all of those negativities from every other area of your body, and place them right at the bottom of your lungs for now. We're going to get rid of them out of our body.

Just get ALL of those negative thoughts and feelings about ANYTHING that's going on in your life right now that may not be serving you well.

At home, at work, with friendships/family, thoughts about yourself…..whatever it is – just put in in the bottom of your lungs.

Now I'd like you to imagine them as the colour 'black'. As you are breathing normally, filling the bottom of your lungs with all of those negative thoughts (that are the colour black) – just visualise them there for a moment, because we're now going to get rid of them.

I'd like you to put the balloon up to your mouth and blow all of that 'black' negativity out into the balloon.

Keep blowing all of it out until you blow up your balloon, so that there's no more left in your lungs – and it's all inside the balloon.

All that 'black' negative air that was in the bottom of your lungs is now inside this balloon.

Now, putting your fingers on the neck of the balloon – just pinch it together so that none escapes yet.

Now as we all count to '3' together, we're going to let the balloons go.

Ready, 1,2,3!!! **(balloons will zoom around the room).**

Now taking a big breath in……inhale all the colours of the rainbow into your body, and filling your lungs and circulating through your body – feeling fresh and vibrant, and full of positive energy.

Just know – that every time you breathe in, you have a choice of what to allow into your body and your mind.

*'Colours' are so much 'lighter' to carry around, and give you a real sense of exhilarating feelings – so choose wisely. And if your thoughts aren't serving you well, just know that you can always **exhale – and let them go.***

And – 'Relax'…and open your eyes….and breathe normally.

Purpose

Resilience / Happiness

This is a simple little technique that uses the senses of the body, imagery, and words – to suggest a way to rid the mind/body of negative thoughts, and replace it with the feeling of positivity.

It shows participants that they are able to have a sense of 'control' over what kind of thoughts can enter their mind, and can freely get rid of them if they no longer want them to be there.

Life Lesson

'If you have good thoughts, they will shine out of your face like sunbeams and you will always look lovely'

-Ronald Dahl-

10.

Guess Who

Approx. Duration

- 20-60 minutes (depending on the size of group)

Resources Required

- Paper
- Pen
- Container

Preparation

The participants are to be seated in a circle, with the container full of the notes inside the circle.

Activity

First, all participants (even the facilitator) are to write down one thing about themselves – that they don't think that anyone else in the group would know. (Eg: I was a champion high-jumper in primary school, or I have a phobia of heights etc).

Participants are to then fold up their statement about themselves and put it in the container provided in the middle of the group.

One by one, each participant will take their turn to randomly pick out a statement, and all members of the group will try to guess who belongs to that statement.

When all have been read out and identified, the participants should discuss what they've learnt.

Purpose

Team Building / Resilience / Confidence

Team members can often spend years around the same people, and not really get to know them.

This can be a fun activity, and also be a good way to open the communication channels further between the groups.

Life Lesson

'*Spending time with people and knowing them, aren't the same thing*'

-Di McMath-

11.

Interesting Commonalities

Approx. Duration

- 40 minutes

Resources Required

- Marker pens
- Large sheets of paper for each group

Preparation

Participants are to get into groups of 3 (maximum groups of 4)

The facilitator may wish to select the groups to make it more interesting, or in an attempt to mix different personalities.

Activity

Participants are to draw 3 large circles interlinking each other, and asked to take approximately 15-20mins to come up with the _most interesting thing that the group all has in common_. The group has to do this by asking and responding to questions. (Eg: Do we all play sport? Soccer? Did you play representative soccer at any stage? – then participants may find out that they all went to the same match of Australia vs. England).

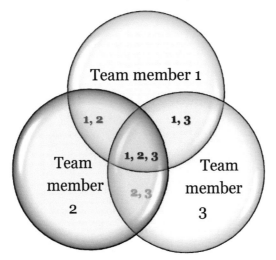

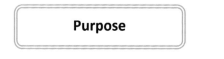

Purpose

Team Building / Leadership Building / Confidence / Self Awareness

A lot of the time we can spend years around the same people in work or through school or even in friendships, and not really *know* the people we are surrounded by!

This exercise encourages participants to get to know each other, and can form connections and bonds that they never knew existed – yet were always there.

It's a great exercise to break down those preconceived ideas that people may have about each other.

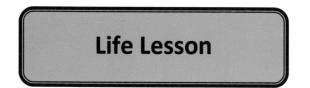

Life Lesson

"Never judge a book by its cover – the best bits are usually on the inside"

-Di McMath-

12.

The Power of Tone and Expression

Approx. Duration

- 20-40 minutes

Resources Required

- Approximately 3-5 picture frames (can be actual frames, or made out of cardboard)
- Permanent marker pen (for cardboard frames) or different 'smiley faces' (approximately A6 size)
- Blu-Tack

Preparation

Each frame has a different theme.

Themes could be: *Angry, Sad, Happy, Serious, Excited, Sarcastic* etc (written on the frames with permanent marker)

Activity

The facilitator is to give examples of saying sentences in different 'tones' whilst standing behind each of the frames.

Emphasis on particular words will create the desired example of each of the frames.

Eg: "Can you please all gather around?"

Angry frame = "CAN YOU **PLEASE** ALL GATHER AROUND!" (Louder voice and angry facial expression)

Sad frame = "Can you **_please_** all gather around?" (quiet voice and sad expression)

Sarcastic = "Can **'_YOU'_** please all gather around?" (emphasis on the 'you' – whilst lifting eyebrows and tilting head)

Participants are to then come up with a sentence that is relevant to their group (Eg: A sentence used in selling a product), and take turns in saying it with the different 'tones' and expressions.

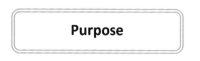

Purpose

Self Awareness / Leadership Building

This activity shows participants how just one slight change of tone with certain words, can have a huge change in how it is interpreted for the receiver. Further steps to the activity can be taken, and role play with various scenarios can be acted out.

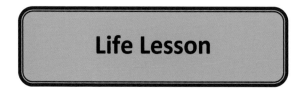

Life Lesson

'10% of conflicts is due to a difference of opinion, 90% is due to the wrong tone of voice.'

-Unknown-

13.

The Compliment Chair

Approx. Duration

- 60 minutes

Resources Required

- Paper
- Pen
- Chairs

Preparation

This activity works well if the participants know each other, yet can still be done if they don't (it can be modified to 'first impressions'). It's an activity on expressing what qualities you like about the other participants, followed by learning to accept a compliment. A great team building exercise, building one's self-esteem, and can even dampen 'conflict' within the group.

Chairs are to be situated in a semicircle with one chair facing the semicircle. The chair facing the others will be known as the 'Compliment Chair'.

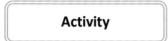

Activity

Each participant writes down a list of all of the people in the group.

Beside each of their names, the participants are to write down the quality or the thing that they most **like** about each person on their list. (Only positive / kind things can be said). (If it's modified to 'first impressions' – things such as they have a friendly 'vibe' about them etc)

When everyone has completed their list, each participant takes turns sitting in the compliment chair, and the only words that the participant in that position is permitted to say is "Thank You". All of the other participants take turns in reading out what they have written about the person in the compliment chair.

Facilitators can then compile the lists by rewriting them so that everyone in the group has their own individual list of qualities that their group likes about them. This can be done over time, and is nice to hand to each group member at the end of the year for them to keep.

Di McMath

Purpose

Self Esteem / Team Building / Resilience / Confidence / Self Awareness / Happiness

This exercise forces participants to source out the 'good' qualities in people, rather than always noticing what they don't like (if conflict within the group dynamics). In turn, it allows all participants to learn to 'accept' compliments rather than shy away or deflect them.

When participants obtain their personalised list of what their team / group like about them, it is a constant reminder that their qualities are valued by other people.

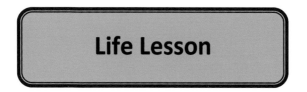

'How you make
others feel about
themselves, says a
lot about you'

- Unknown -

Keeping Dreams Alive

Approx. Duration

- 10-15 minutes

Resources Required

- Balloons (enough for each participant)
- Permanent marker pens
- Upbeat music (***see appendix for a suggested Play list**)

Preparation

Participants are to have an area with no hazards (eg: tables/chairs, trip hazards, ceiling fans etc).

Activity

Participants are to blow up a balloon and write one of their goals/wishes on it with a permanent marker pen.

Whilst upbeat music is played, participants are instructed to try and keep all of the balloons in the air – without them landing on the floor.

If any fall to the ground – they are to be picked up and continue to try and keep them in the air.

Following the short activity, lead into a discussion about what the participants learnt from that activity.

Purpose

Self Esteem / Team Building / Goal Setting / Resilience / Confidence / Happiness

To keep ones goals and dreams *alive,* **energy** is needed.

If you seem to hit rock bottom whilst trying to keep your goals and dreams alive, simply pick up where you left off – and keep going!

If *someone else* is struggling to keep theirs alive….do what you can to help them!

If your dream 'pops'…just simply make another dream!

Have fun whilst trying to keep your dream alive! When you are enjoying yourself, it's easier to make the effort!

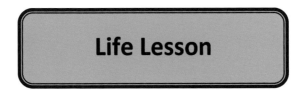

'A dreamer is one who can only find his way by moonlight, and his punishment is that he sees the dawn before anyone else.'

-Oscar Wilde-

Pin the 'Star' on the Target

Approx. Duration

- 20-30 minutes

Resources Required

- A dart board / target board drawn onto a large piece of paper

- Blu-tack or sticky tape

- Blindfold or toy glasses with the lens coloured in with Black permanent marker.

- Star shapes – Print the sheet provided and cut out the stars. **(*see appendix for Bonus Downloadable sheets)**

The provided sheet looks like this :

Preparation

Ensure that there is an appropriate amount of space for this activity (free from hazards etc).

This activity is played like 'Pin the tail on the Donkey',   except the idea is to try to stick your 'star' on the 'bullseye' of the target.

Activity

Participants are each given a star shape, and asked to write their name on the front of it.

Taking turns, participants are blindfolded and spun around 3 x.

They then try to pin their star on the bullseye of the dart /target board

After all participants have had their turn, the facilitator is to explain about the importance of being 'clear and specific' with what their goal is.

Knowing 'WHAT' they want, and placing emphasis on the 'WHY' they want it (What's their purpose for wanting it? What will it give them when they reach it?)

Participants are then encouraged to specifically and clearly write down their goals, and their purpose for wanting them.

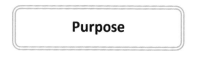

Purpose

Goal Setting

If an individual or group is not specific and clear on what goals they are after, they will have trouble reaching their target. The 'Why' (Purpose) is what will *drive* (motivate) them to get there.

This activity can be followed up with creating an 'action plan' on how to achieve the goals.

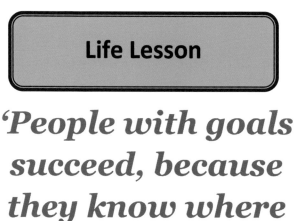

Life Lesson

'People with goals succeed, because they know where they are going. It's as simple as that'

Earl Nightingale

16.

Burst Your OWN Bubbles!

- 5-10 minutes

- Bubble mixture for all participants

An outdoor space is probably the best place to conduct this activity

Participants are to think of their *wishes* that they would like to come true. Whilst blowing their bubbles, think of each wish individually – and *imagine* blowing the wish into it.

When each participant pops their own bubble, they are to *imagine* that their wish is dispersed into the universe.

Purpose

Goal Setting / Resilience / Self Esteem

So often, we can take things to heart and let other people's fears and anxieties destroy our own wishes and goals. In other words – they can 'burst our bubble'. This well-known metaphor has a negative connotation to it.

In this activity, participants are able to 'reframe' the metaphor into a more positive and empowering meaning – and take a sense of control over bursting it themselves.

Don't let anyone else burst your bubble….you burst your own, but have fun doing it!

Free it, and place your order with the universe!

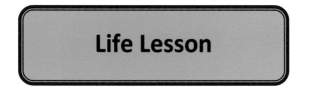

'I wish for you a day of joy and happiness, a day when you feel like blowing bubbles just for the sheer joy of seeing them float into the sky, carrying your dreams towards the heavens.'

-Unknown-

Vision Boards

Approx. Duration

- 90 -120 minutes

Resources Required

- Large poster size cardboard
- Magazines
- Photos (brought in by participants) that can be cut up and glued
- Scissors
- Glue

Preparation

Lots of floor/desk space will be required

Activity

Participants are encouraged to *let their mind run free*, and be creative and cut things out of magazines that they would like to have in their lives.

The more detail the better – eg: letters can be cut out to create specific words that the individual would like to attract into their lives. Photos with their faces can be stuck onto pictures cut out of the magazines to create the visualisation of being in that particular environment etc.

Purpose

Goal Setting / Confidence / Self Awareness / Happiness

The mind cannot tell the difference between something that's vividly imagined, and what's real, therefore by creating a *vision board* of things that you would *like* to attract into your life, we are attempting to *trick* the brain into thinking not only that it's possible, but that it's already real.

Where focus goes, energy flows - therefore the more someone focuses on their vision board on a regular basis, the more they will become both unconsciously and consciously aware of opportunities that can help them move towards the things in their life that they wish to have.

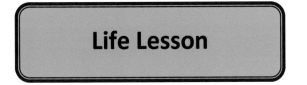

Life Lesson

'It's a terrible thing to see, but have no vision'

-Helen Keller-

#

Achieving Success

Approx. Duration

- 5-10 minutes

Resources Required

- Whiteboard or PowerPoint for discussion at the end of the activity.

Preparation

Each participant is to stand in a space where they will have at least an arms distance from the person next to them.

Activity

The facilitator asks participants to lift their right arm with their pointer finger out in front of them, and turn around clockwise as far as they can comfortably go – and notice where their finger ended up.

Bring their pointed finger back to the front and put their arm down by their side.

Participants are then asked to close their eyes and *imagine* that they are lifting their same arm and finger up and turning around clockwise – but this time going a little bit further than the last time. Then *imagine* coming back around to the front and their arm and finger come down by their side.

Next, participants are to *imagine* that they are really flexible and have arms like 'Mr Tickle' (out of the Mr Men characters – or choose a character that will represent 'flexibility' for the group).

Still keeping their eyes closed, participants are to **imagine** that they are lifting their same arm and finger up, turning clockwise past the first point that they reached, then past the second point they reached, and now *ALL* the way around 360° so that they are now twisted and facing forward again...........and *unravel.*

Now, participants are to open their eyes and repeat the process again; lifting their right arm up in front of them, finger pointed, and turning clockwise as far as they can comfortably go.

Now, coming back to their original stance, discuss how many participants went further the second time, than they did the first time.

You should see an increase of approximately 25% in most participants.

Purpose

Self Esteem / Goal Setting / Confidence / Self Awareness

The brain cannot tell the difference between something that's vividly imagined or what's real, therefore participants have essentially *tricked* their brain into thinking that they have done it before – so it's not only possible, but they can do better than they first thought.

The key was....*They saw their results in advance.*

That gave them a greater **belief** or certainty that they were able to achieve it, therefore that increased their **potential.**

The increase in potential, allowed them to take greater **action,** and therefore they got better **results.**

Getting better results reinforces their **belief** and so on.

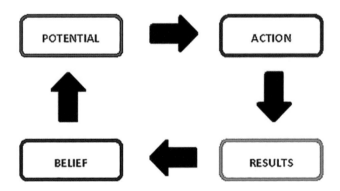

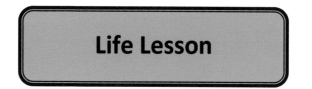

Life Lesson

'If you develop the absolute sense of certainty that powerful beliefs provide, then you can get yourself to accomplish virtually anything. Including those things that other people are certain are impossible.'

-Anthony Robbins-

19.

Lead with Dancing

Approx. Duration

- 5 minutes

Resources Required

- Upbeat music (***see appendix for a suggested Play list).**

Preparation

Participants are to either be standing in one big group or break into smaller groups (preferably about 3-4 people). Create an appropriate space in the room (away from furniture)

Activity

Dance music is played at random times to create an upbeat atmosphere within the group.

The facilitator states that one person is to lead the group with a certain type of dance move and all others are to copy that particular person within the group.

After approximately 30 seconds with one person leading the dance move of each group, the facilitator directs the groups to 'change' – and the next person begins to lead the group with a different dance move.

For adults, different themes of dancing can be used (eg: sexy dance, break dance, feminine dance etc)

> **Purpose**

Self Esteem / Team Building / Resilience / Confidence / Leadership Building

This is a fun and light hearted way to change the atmosphere within the room into being fun and uplifted. It also gives participants a chance to feel what it's like to be able to lead the group in a fun and entertaining way.

'Leaders become
great, not because
of their power, but
of their ability to
empower others'

-John Maxwell-

20.

Which Hat Will You Wear?

Approx. Duration

- 40-60 minutes

Resources Required

- Approximately 5 picture frames (actual frames, or cardboard ones that are decorated can be used) OR

  Hats (approximately 5 different ones)

- Paper

- Pen

Preparation

This activity could be implemented for many different reasons. If there is conflict within the group, failing to meet targets, teambuilding strategies etc.

The facilitator would need to be prepared with a set of scenarios and questions for their specific need.

Activity

Discussion about each individual having 'different personalities' (wearing *'different hats')* in different situations (explained below).

Each participant is to write down all of their personalities/hats that they perceive they wear, and the positive attributes and the negative attributes that those particular personalities have.

Eg: Lily – the 'mum'; loving and fun, but can also be impatient. Lily – the 'lover'; loyal, caring, compassionate and loving, but can also be too demanding and jealous.

(Encourage participants to think of as many attributes as they can for each one).

Then, the facilitator asks for a volunteer to introduce all of their personalities/hats they wear, and explain a bit about each one.

If they have 5 personalities/hats, then there are 5 other participants that are holding the frames or hats for them.

As the facilitator gives the participant scenarios relating to what issues need to be improved within the group, the participant is asked to decide which frame or hat that they could stand behind or wear, that could assist in giving a better approach or input into the solution.

Eg: "If someone was bullying your friend / colleague, which personality / hat could you wear that could best help the situation?

What could you do?

What could you say?"

Other questions that the facilitator could discuss with the group are things like:

"What hat do you commonly wear?

Do you like it?

Which one do you like best?

Which one do you think could get a better outcome if you let it step up in this situation instead of the one that you normally let run things?"

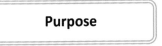

Purpose

Self Awareness / Leadership Building / Resilience / Confidence

A lot of the time we aren't aware of our different personalities that we portray in different situations.

When we see our personality as a whole, instead of realising each individual one's qualities and weaknesses – we can tend to get confused and angry at ourselves for reacting or responding the way we sometimes do.

With separating them to be able to see what each one has to offer, it can be very helpful to choose the right one for that situation rather than involuntarily allowing our dominant personality to step in and possibly be detrimental to the situation.

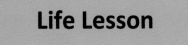

Life Lesson

'Love all of your personality traits, and thank them for what they have to offer.

Become friends with all of them, because none of them can shape your soul on their own"

- Di McMath-

The Power of Journals

Approx. Duration

- 5-10 minutes

Resources Required

- Notebooks / Journals
- Pen
- Soothing music (optional) **(*see appendix for a suggested Play list).**

Preparation

At a consistent time of day (eg: start of the day for 'Gratitude Journals', end of the day for 'Journals'), ask participants to take a few moments to write in their journals.

Activity

Gratitude Journal: (preferably at the start of the session). Participants are encouraged to take a few moments to write down at least 3 things that they are grateful for in their life ***in detail***. Eg: I am so grateful for 'my wonderful husband who always knows how to make me laugh when I am stressed', as opposed to just writing 'My husband'.

Journaling: (preferably at the end of the session). Participants are encouraged to take a few moments to write down the things that made them feel good from that day.

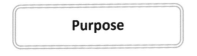

Purpose

Self Awareness / Happiness

Research has shown that there are things we should do on a consistent basis to increase our happiness in the present (which in turn, unlocks the key to happiness). Two of these things are: *'Gratitude and Journaling'.*

Gratitude: Noting down at least 3 things to be grateful for every day, teaches our minds to **look** for the positive things in the world first, rather than the negative.

Journaling: Writing down at least 1 positive experience you've had in the past 24hrs, allows your brain to relive it!

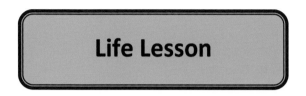

'It's not happiness
that brings us
gratitude, it's
gratitude that
brings us
happiness'

– Unknown-

22.

Achievement Boards

Approx. Duration

- 45-60 minutes

Resources Required

- Large poster cardboard
- Magazines
- Scissors
- Glue
- Coloured felt tip pens or paints
- Notepad and pen

Preparation

Participants are to write down times in their lives (or it can more specific - like the past year), and list all of their *achievements* that they can remember throughout that time. It could be something like 'riding my pushbike without training wheels at 5yrs old', or 'graduating university' etc.

Activity

Then, participants are to create a poster that portrays their list (or whatever bits of the list that they like) in a positive and uplifting way. (Eg: Posters may be done as a 'timeline', recognising achievements at various times of the participants' lives.)

Facilitators / teachers may even like to interrupt the class at times with instructions to "Turn to the person next to you and read out one of your achievements – then 'High 5' them and shout "We're awesome!!"

Purpose

Self Esteem / Resilience / Confidence / Self Awareness / Happiness

So often, people can be caught up in being disappointed that they aren't reaching their goals quick enough, or they *compare* themselves to others.

This activity allows the participant to metaphorically hit the 'pause' button of life, and review what has already been achieved.

A lot of the times, goals have been achieved without allowing for self-recognition – and giving ourselves a pat on the back!

The key to this activity is to guide the participant to recognise what they perceive as *small* achievements – as really being quite significant events.

Life Lesson

'Enjoy the little
things in life, for
one day you may
look back and
realise that they
were the big things'

-Robert Brault-

Little Jar of Fulfilment

Approx. Duration

- 30 – 40 minutes

Resources Required

- Participants are asked to bring in their own plain glass jar
- Ribbon
- Small notepads or post-it notes
- Labels (either made of cardboard to tie around the jar, or sticky labels)
- Pens

Preparation

There are several occasions that this can be done for.

Facilitators can decide what is suitable for the group.

Activity

Participants are to each have a clear glass jar, a pen and a small notepad. Each participant picks someone whom they will be giving the jar to once it is full.

The reasoning behind each jar can be different.

Examples can be:

- Reasons why I love you
- Reasons why you're my friend
- Reasons why I like you
- Reasons why you make me smile
- Reasons why you're valued in our office

Etc etc etc

One piece of paper is used for each 'reason', and then folded and put into the jar. When the jar is full, put the lid on and tie a ribbon around it. Attach a label with the name of the jar (Eg: 'Reasons why I love you)

Jars can be done as a group activity also. For example – sending encouragement to a classmate / friend / colleague who may be unwell.

Purpose

Self Esteem / Confidence / Self Awareness / Happiness

So often, life can go by and we haven't expressed how much someone really means to us.

These little jars of fulfilment, give exactly what they are called....'fulfilment'.

So often, society can become so stressed from feeling obliged to give 'materialistic' gifts.

Stresses come from many things - from the monetary factors, to the feeling of the gift not being 'good enough', to being in the 'comparison' mode with other gifts that are given etc.

However, when you 'fill someone up' from the *inside* (intrinsic motivation) with positive words of appreciation and heartfelt sentiments, the effects are deep and longer lasting.

It not only has positive effects on the receiver of the jar, but it also has positive effects on the 'giver' of it too, and hopefully starts a 'ripple effect' when the idea is spread to others.

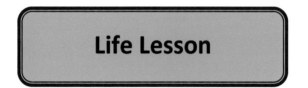

Life Lesson

'It's not how much we give, but how much love we put into giving'

- Mother Teresa-

Creative Questioning

- Anywhere from 5mins up to 60mins (facilitator discretion)

Resources Required

If the activity is for children then use

- A bag of brightly coloured small plastic children's balls (eg: The ones for in a ball pit)
- Permanent marker pen
- Brightly decorated bucket to keep the balls in

Or for adults use:

- A clear jar – labelled with the activity name
- Pen and paper

Preparation

This activity is great for 'icebreakers' and to get participants to stretch their mind and think laterally. This is great at random times within a session – to change the group energy.

Activity

Questions can be written on the plastic balls, or pieces of paper – and drawn out at random.

Use questions that encourage the participant to *think* and explore their mind for answers that they may not be consciously aware of, but just need the right question to bring it out in them.

Some possible questions are provided on the next page.

(* see appendix for more examples of suitable questions).

Suggestions for questions:

How do you go about fixing a problem? – What steps do you take?

What is something that you're looking forward to?

What is one experience that really changed your life in a positive way?

If you could wave a magic wand and have things the way you would like it, what would you wish for?

Purpose

Self Esteem / Team Building / Leadership Building / Goal Setting / Resilience / Confidence / Self Awareness / Happiness

This activity *stretches* the mind to think beyond day to day thinking.

It starts conversation, and encourages lateral thinking.

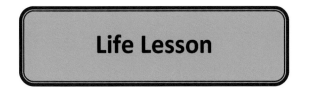

'Questions wake people up. They prompt new ideas. They show people new places, new ways of doing things'

-Michael Marquardt-

Emotional Reactions

Approx. Duration

- 20-40 minutes

Resources Required

- Pieces of paper with one word on each (emotions can be varied to suit the group)
  - Anger
  - Sadness
  - Happy
  - Frustration
  - Determined

  (These can be printed and laminated if you wish)
- Blu-tack

- List of scenarios (that relate and are suitable for their group)

Preparation

The pieces of paper are to be Blu-tacked in different areas of the room.

Activity

Facilitators are to read out, one by one, a list of common scenarios that may occur within the environment.

Eg: "Another person gets picked for something over you. What emotion would you tend to react with?" or,

"Someone you care about has been diagnosed with cancer – what emotion would tend to dominate you?"

Participants (already standing) are to move to the signed area with the emotion that they would honestly react with.

Once participants have moved to an area, the facilitator initiates a short discussion about the reasons behind the participant choosing that response.

Then questions them as to what they would have to ask themselves, to be able to see the situation in a positive light and choose a different emotion? (eg: more positive).

Purpose

Leadership Building / Resilience / Self Awareness

This exercise can give participants a realisation of what emotion they commonly respond with if situations don't always go the way they've planned.

By the facilitator using guided questioning, participants can see the benefits of reacting in a more positive way.

Seeing things from a different perspective.

Questions such as: "What do you think could happen if you stepped into the happy area?

Yes – it may be a terrible thing that's just happened, but what if you said to yourself: What do I need to do from this point onwards, to make myself and others happy?"

In doing this activity, it can provide the participant with *options* of different emotions, and allows them to see that they are in control of how they respond/react.

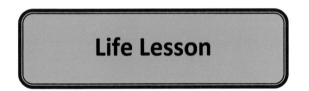

Life Lesson

'We may not have control over what happens, but we can control how we react to it'

-*Unknown*-

APPENDIX

Your Bonus downloadable sheets for the Activities can be found at the link below.

You will need the password **ICEB25** to access the download page.

http://www.platinumpotential.com.au/book/bonus-content-password-required/

The downloadable sheets are as follows:

- "I AM" sheet for Activity 1.
- Disempowering to Empowering Statement Worksheet for Activity 3
- Balance Sheet of Life Worksheet for Activity 8
- Stars Cut-out Sheet for Activity 15

Creative Questioning

Examples of random questions

1. What steps do you take to fix a problem?

2. If you could have dinner with someone famous – who would it be and what would you ask them?

3. Who inspires you and why?

4. What is the kindest thing that anyone has ever done for you?

5. What would you do if money didn't exist?

6. What is a quote that you love?

7. If you had a magic wand, how would you use it?

8. Imagining you were at the end of your life, and you could give nothing but one bit of advice to others – what would it be?

9. What is the number one thing that makes you happy?

10. What could be a 'Random Act of Kindness' that you could do for others? – (Individually or as a group).

11. Who are you proud of and why? (In your immediate group, and/or outside the group).

12. Who is the kindest person you know and why?

13. What is your favourite childhood memory?

14. What is your funniest memory?

15. What experience has changed your life in a positive way? (This can be modified to being specifically about the group).

16. If you could go anywhere in the world, where would it be and why?

17. What is the weirdest thing you have in common with the person next to you?

18. What can you do to make someone laugh?

19. What is the funniest thing you remember happening at school?

20. What is one (1) thing that you could do to make someone else's day awesome?

21. Who do you need to apologise to?

22. What is the quality that you most like in a friend?

23. If your life was a book - what kind of story has it been so far, and what kind of story would you like the rest of it to be?

24. What is something that you are looking forward to?

25. If you had to name an animal that best describes you, what animal would it be and why?

26. What is your favourite family (or friends) tradition?

27. What are your top 5 values (things that are most important to you)?

28. What would you do if you knew you couldn't fail?

29. What is the number one (1) thing that gets you motivated?

30. What do you love about winter?

31. What would your *perfect day* look like?

32. Which one of your personalities do you *like* the most?

33. If you could speak to your 5yr old *self*, what would you say?

Music List

Ideas for Inspirational music (mellow and upbeat)

1. Forrest Gump Suite (Excerpt)
   Steven Bear – *Beautiful Movie Themes for Piano Solo*

2. Practical Magic: Amas Veritas (The Legend)
   Steven Bear – *Beautiful Movie Themes for Piano Solo*

3. Devi Prayer
   Anthony Robbins: Sacred Music Inspired by the World's Great Faiths

4. Canon in D
   Johann Pachelbel *(Sharon O'Connors – Romance)*

5. Northwind
   Tony O'Connonor -*Mariner*

6. Now We Are Free
   (Soundtrack from the Motion Picture 'Gladiator')
   Lisa Gerrard, Gavin Greenaway, The Lyndhurst Orchestra, Bruce Fowler, Yvonne S. Moriarty, Walt Fowler, Ladd McIntosh, Elizabeth Finch, Jack Smalley and Hans Zimmer

7. You Raise Me Up
   Josh Groban

8. Let It Be
   The Beatles

9. Walk of Life
   Dire Straits – *Sultans of Swing: The very best of Dire Straits*

10. Man in the Mirror
    Michael Jackson

11. Smile
    Uncle Kracker

12. Just the Way You Are
    Bruno Mars

13. We Are the World -
    U.S.A. for Africa

14. Beautiful Day
    U2

15. Take Me to the Clouds Above
    LMC vs. U2

16. I Got a Feeling
    Black Eyed Peas

17. Firework
    Katy Perry

18. What a Wonderful World
    Israel Kamakawiwo'ole - *Somewhere over the rainbow*

19. Wake Me Up
    Avicii

20. Happy
    Pharrell Williams *(From Despicable Me 2)*

REFERENCES

Activity 1:

- Inspired and adapted from the teachings of Hay. L.L, (1984) *You Can Heal Your Life*, Hay House. (and DVD).
- Adapted from the teachings of Debbie Hogg (Life Coach) – *Inspirational Living Retreat.*

Activity 2:

- Inspired and adapted from the teachings of Hay. L.L, (1984) *You Can Heal Your Life*, Hay House. (and DVD).

Activity 3:

- Inspired and adapted from the teachings of Anthony Robbins – *Unleash the Power Within*, & *Date with Destiny* events.

Activity 4:

- Parts of this activity was inspired by the movie *Up In the Air* – starring George Clooney.

Activity 5:

- This activity was adapted from the Anthony Robbins event – *Date with Destiny* event.

Activity 6:

- Adapted from the teachings of Dr Masuru Emoto - *http://www.masaru-emoto.net/english/water-crystal.html* and *http://www.youtube.com/watch?v=iu9P167HLsw*

Activity 7:

- Inspired by the teachings of Neuro Linguistic Programming.
- Parts of this activity was inspired by the movie *Up In the Air* – starring George Clooney.

Activity 8:

- Adapted from Anthony Robbins – *Unleash the Power Within* event.

Activity 9:

- Inspired by the teachings of Neuro Linguistic Programming.

Activity 10:

- The author had no influences to any references for this activity.

Activity 11:

- Adapted from the teachings of Mr Geoffrey Williamson – *Former National Sales Training Manager & Sales Capability Leader of Lion Breweries, New Zealand*

Activity 12:

- Inspired by the teachings of Neuro Linguistic Programming.

Activity 13:

- Adapted from the teachings of Mr Geoffrey Williamson – *Former Sales Training Manager of Lion Nathan Breweries, New Zealand*

Activity 14:

- Inspired by the teachings of Neuro Linguistic Programming.
- Inspired by the teachings of Gordon,J (2007) *The Energy Bus,* Wiley Publishing.

Activity 15:

- Inspired and adapted from Anthony Robbins – *Date with Destiny* event.

Activity 16:

- Inspired by my daughter, Ella Claire Exley, 2015.

Activity 17:

- Inspired by Rhonda Byrne; DVD - *The Secret*.
- Assaraf, J. (2008) *The Vision Board Book,* Beyond Words Publishing.
- Inspired by the teachings of Oprah Winfrey.

Activity 18:

- Inspired by Anthony Robbins interview with Frank Kerns and John Reese
  https://www.youtube.com/watch?v=oImIuAvkUMo

Activity 19:

- Inspired by Anthony Robbins – *Unleash the Power Within* event.

Activity 20:

- Inspired by Anthony Robbins – *Date with Destiny* event.

Activity 21:

- Inspired by the teachings of Oprah Winfrey.
- Inspired and adapted by Shawn Achor TED talk: http://www.ted.com/talks/shawn_achor_the_happy_secret_to_better_work

Activity 22:

- Inspired by the teachings of Anthony Robbins, and Marie Forleo.

Activity 23:

- Inspired and adapted from 365 days grateful – the documentary https://www.facebook.com/video.php?v=787801121281706&set=vr.787801121281706&type=2&theater

Activity 24:

- Inspired from the teachings of Life Coaching.

Activity 25:

- Inspired by the teachings of Anthony Robbins.

BIBLIOGRAPHY

Becker, D. (2008). *50 Life Skills to Ensure Kids Stay in School, Off Drugs and Out of Trouble.* London: Continuum International Publishing Group.

Canfield, J. (2007). *Teachers of The Secret – Recorded Live in Toronto.* Audio CD: Power Within Inc.

Gordon, J. (2007). *The Energy Bus.* New Jersey: John Wiley and Sons, Inc.

Gordon, J. (2008). *The No Complaining Rule.* New Jersey: John Wiley & Sons, Inc.

Gordon, J. (2011). *The Seed.* New Jersey: John Wiley and Sons, Inc.

Gordon, J. (2012). *The Positive Dog.* New Jersey: John Wiley and Sons, Inc.

Gordon, J. (2014). *The Carpenter.* New Jersey: John Wiley and Sons, Inc.

Hay, L. (1984). *You Can Heal Your Life.* NSW: Hay House Pty Ltd.

Nichols. L (2007). *Teachers of The Secret – Recorded Live in Toronto.* Audio CD: Power Within Inc.

Robbins, A. (1991). *Awaken the Giant Within.* New York: Summit Books.

Robbins, A. (2010). *The New Money Masters – Interview with Marie Forleo.* Audio CD & DVD.

ABOUT THE AUTHOR

Di McMath is a qualified Life Coach and Neuro-Linguistic Programming (NLP) Practitioner, who has a passion to help educate others on *how to live their best lives.*

Driven by the quest to enrich her own personal development after experiencing several life 'challenges', Di has studied the teachings of many of the world's top leaders in their field including Anthony Robbins, Oprah Winfrey, Louise L. Hay, Marie Forleo, Sir. Richard Branson, Robert Kiyosaki, Dr. Wayne Dyer, Jack Canfield, and Lisa Nichols just to name a few. Her interests are in the area of self-help, personal development, life coaching, positive psychology, 'human needs' psychology, wealth creation, and spirituality.

Ultimately inspired by the teachings of her mentor – Leading Peak Performance Coach 'Anthony Robbins', Di graduated from his Mastery University in 2012 and then went on to gaining her coaching qualifications through the Life Coaching Academy, Gold Coast, Australia.

Di has an extensive background in pre-hospital emergency care, having spent almost 15 years predominantly as an Advanced Care Paramedic within the Queensland Ambulance Service. This has also complemented her skills as a Registered Nurse, where she still spends some of her time working.

Di founded 'Platinum Potential' and now conducts seminars and workshops, as well as one-on-one coaching, on 'maintaining healthy mindsets' through various coaching and NLP techniques. With her 'Emergency Services' background, she has a keen interest to enrich the lives of emergency personnel through her inspirational coaching and compassion.

Website: www.platinumpotential.com.au or

Email: di@platinumpotential.com.au

Di lives in the Gold Coast hinterland in Qld Australia, with her partner Ric and their beautiful daughter Ella.

Other Books from Dreamstone Publishing

Dreamstone publishes books in a wide variety of categories – here are some of our other bestselling books:-

The Father Balance
How YOU, as a Father, can successfully build a career and, at the same time, still keep your marriage and family together !

By Leith Adams

Business Strategy :
12 Steps to Business Sanity
How to Optimize Your Profits and Your Time, Grow Your Business and Get Your Life Back Too!

By Kim Lambert

From The Inside Out:
Breakthrough Strategies for
Mastering Your Finances:
What YOU Need to Know NOW to Change Your Relationship with Money and Achieve Financial Freedom

By Linda Binns